You Look Awfully
Like the Queen

You Look Awfully Like the Queen

WIT AND WISDOM FROM
THE HOUSE OF WINDSOR

THOMAS BLAIKIE

ILLUSTRATED BY GILL TYLER

FOURTH ESTATE • *London*

First published in Great Britain in 2002 by
Fourth Estate
A Division of HarperCollins*Publishers*
77–85 Fulham Palace Road,
London W6 8JB
www.4thestate.com

A catalogue record for this book is available from the
British Library

ISBN 0-00-714874-7

Designed by Geoff Green, Cambridge CB4 5RA
Printed in Great Britain by
Clays Ltd, St Ives plc

Acknowledgements

~

I am very grateful to those who have helped me tremendously in person: Tom Ades, Carol Anderson, Larry Ashmead, Adam Bager, Kate Balmforth, Lady Freda Berkeley, Tamsyn Blaikie, Michael Bloch, Catherine Blyth, Jennifer Bowen, Antonio Carluccio, Reverend Stephen Coles, Michael De-la-Noy, Patric Dickinson, Derek Granger, Digby Green, Geoff Green, Maggie Hambling, Selina Hastings, Ian Hay, Tim Hely Hutchinson, Mary Hendy, Gregory Hayman, Philip Hensher, Alan Hollinghurst, Joe Hunter, Sarah Hunter, Tina Jefferis MBE, Francis King, Katharine MacDonogh, Rick Mather, Kitty Morris, Patrick O'Connor, Peter Parker, Kenneth Partridge, Christopher Potter, Kit Reading, Tony Scotland, Ivan Seery, Sean Swallow, Robert Tiffler, Gill Tyler, Warris Vianni, Richard Walker, Jill White OBE, James Woollcombe CBE, Phoebe Woollcombe; to those who don't wish to be mentioned, and to those whose information has been most useful: Theo Aronson, Jennie Bond, Craig Brown, Alan Clark, Colin Clark, Lesley Cunliffe, Cynthia Gladwyn, Kitty Kelley, Robert Lacey, James Lees-Milne, Elizabeth Longford, Ann Morrow, Laurence Olivier, Kenneth Rose, Gore Vidal, Woodrow Wyatt, Philip Ziegler.

Foreword

'*H*ow come you know so much about the Royal Family?' people often ask me. The question is intended as a challenge. Nowadays an interest in the Monarchy has to be justified. As a child I only wanted to hear about people who lived in large houses and had masses of money. I was engrossed in a life of Queen Mary at the age of nine and later, while other boys at school were leafing through *Autocar* or setting fire to things, I was slaving in the pottery room on a head of that same queen – capturing her marcel wave in clay was a nightmare. Even now, at forty-four, it's a comfort to wonder what the Queen might be doing at the same moment as I am dusting or washing up and still almost impossible to accept her parallel existence in the same universe.

Barking mad, you might say. Well, I have another alarming symptom. While compiling this book, I found that my memory for all the little details about the Royal Family that I have ever read or heard is extraordinarily retentive. Often I would say to a friend, 'You remember when you told me about the Queen hunting for a hat at Buckingham Palace or that time she found the footmen eating her chocolates …?' and they would look blank. I will never be able to understand how they could have forgotten. This perhaps explains, among other things, why I have been able to include so many previously unpublished stories here.

On a more serious note, it *is* difficult to explain the allure of Royalty. Judging by the response to the death of the Queen Mother there are many who know that the killjoy anti-monarchists have got it wrong; on the other hand, the era of uncritical worship is over. I hope that this book reflects the freer and more complex way we feel about the Royal Family now. At times we might want to revel in their strange *Alice in Wonderland* world where they seem simultaneously down to earth and utterly regal, at others we are more sober – appreciating, especially in the Queen's case, true wit and style and an engaging and distinctive personality. Whatever the truth, let's hope they are never replaced by some colourless figure elevated drearily on 'merit'. Long may they reign over us!

Gracious Me

$\backsim$

$\mathcal{A}$t a Tuesday audience Tony Blair raised the subject of what he called 'the Golden Jubilee'. '*My* Golden Jubilee,' the Queen gently corrected.

On a 1990s State Visit to the Caribbean, the Queen stopped off at the Cayman Islands, which is a tax-haven where every hotel is of unimaginable luxury. At the press reception she said, 'I'm so glad we've got the Yacht with us this time [referring to

the Royal Yacht *Britannia*]. I seem to remember the last time we came here we had to stay in a guest house.'

*A*n escort commander allowed his horse to block the crowd's view of the Queen once too often. From inside the carriage, the Queen said, 'Actually, Captain, I think it's me they've come to see.'

*T*he French government gave a dinner at the Louvre for the Queen during her State Visit of the early 1950s. As they munched their hors d'oeuvres, the Queen revealed that she had never visited the museum before. 'So,' somebody said, 'you've never seen the Mona Lisa.' The Queen admitted that she had not. The next thing anyone knew, the picture was brought into the dining room and left propped up on a chair for the Queen to study at her leisure.

Lady Elwyn Jones hosted a reception for the Pearly Kings and Queens at the House of Lords in the 1970s. One of the Pearly Queens arrived late and rather confused. She approached Lady Elwyn Jones. 'The bus was terrible,' she sighed. 'I'm over eighty. I can't get into my costume any more but I've brought these dolls instead ...' She held up a miniature Pearly King and Queen, slipping her arm around the person standing next to Lady Elwyn Jones. 'I supposed I've missed the Queen Mother. But, perhaps, Lady Elwyn Jones, you could give her these when you next see her.' 'Why don't you give them to her yourself?' said Lady Elwyn Jones, indicating the person the elderly Pearly Queen was inadvertently hugging. It was the Queen Mother. 'Oh my gawd,' exclaimed the old lady, and sank almost to the floor in an arthritic curtsy. 'No, no,' said the Queen Mother, 'you must get up at once. We Queens of East and West have always been equals.'

The Queen's French is the best of any woman in England, as crisp and neat as her clothing. In 1999, she was subject to a hoax telephone call from a Canadian broadcaster posing as the prime minister of Canada. She behaved impeccably, observing every constitutional nicety, and when the hoaxer suggested that they speak in French she was quite unfazed. 'Bon, allez,' she rapped out in triumph.

In 1958 the practice of presenting debutantes at Court was finally dropped. It was really too absurdly snobbish and outdated. But Princess Margaret took a different view. 'We had to put a stop to it,' she said. 'Every tart in London was getting in.'

During the war the Queen Mother got wind that none of the treasures had been evacuated from Apsley House, the London home of the Duke of Wellington. She informed the then duchess, 'I'm coming round at eleven with a van to take them to Frogmore.' At eleven sharp a van drew up, the King and Queen appeared and Her Majesty marched around the rooms, picking out all the valuable items and making a list in pencil.

*I*n Venice in 1984, the Queen Mother remained utterly serene and unflappable as her launch began to take in water. In fact, her lady-in-waiting had the greatest difficulty in getting her out before it sank entirely.

*P*eter Ustinov recalls the extraordinary graciousness of the Queen Mother in the face of some nasty students at Dundee University. She picked up the strips of loo paper they had thrown at her and returned them, saying, 'Are these yours? Did you mean to leave them there? Wouldn't you like them back?'

Late in the day at the Cheltenham Races, it is not unusual for quite a few people to be blind drunk, and once somebody in the company of the Queen Mother was very far gone. 'I have the most marvellous friends,' she said to anyone who approached. Then there was the slightest, dipping pause. 'You probably wouldn't recognise some of them.'

When Michael Fagan intruded into her bedroom in 1982, the Queen's long experience of being a queen is probably what saved the day. She was superbly poised and managed to engage the disturbed man in conversation until she had the brainwave of offering him a cigarette, which gave her an excuse to get out of the room. (It has never been explained why cigarettes are available in the royal bedroom area.) After the terrific strain of the occasion, the Queen sought relief in doing imitations of the cockney chamber maid coming upon the scene. For days afterwards Her Majesty was going about the Palace, saying, 'Bloody 'ell, ma'am, what's 'e doin' in 'ere?'

The Queen Mother's skill in diplomacy was put to the test in her own garden at Clarence House when a group of American students were brought to visit by the Reverend Victor Stock. It was at the time of the Watergate scandal. One of the students *would* keep asking the Queen Mother if she thought President Nixon was guilty. At first she asked the Reverend Stock to explain the role of the constitutional monarchy in Britain. But it was useless. All the student had to say, in the manner of students, was,

'But, Your Majesty, do you think he did it?'
So the Queen Mother prepared herself for
a pronouncement. She became vatic and
distant. Finally she said, 'If I were the president of the United States, I would look in
the bag from time to time.' With that, she
disappeared in a cloud of organdie sweet
pea prints, leaving her listeners gasping at
her wisdom. But the Reverend Stock says
that he always wondered what on earth she
meant.

Queen Mary often asked, 'How's your
poor mother?' or 'How's your poor daughter?' In fact she used this adjective 'poor' so
frequently that people began to wonder to
whom it did not apply. Eventually somebody cracked it. 'Poor' meant anybody who
wasn't royal.

The Chairman of the Milk Marketing
Board was showing the Queen around an
artificial insemination unit when her eye

was caught by something unpleasant in a jar. 'What's that?' she inquired. 'It's a cow's vagina, ma'am.' The Queen didn't blink. *'Ask a silly question!'* she said.

*E*verybody knows that Royal occasions of any kind mean a great deal of waiting. At the Queen's Coronation even the peers had to be in place hours in advance. So the Prince of Wales rather put his foot in it when he arrived at a ceremonial occasion in Cornwall where Girl Guides were beautifully lined up to greet him. He said to Mrs Annette Bowen, the County Commissioner for the Guides, 'Have the Guides been waiting long?' Without hesitation, she replied, 'What do you think, sir?' Luckily he saw her point at once. *'Ask a silly question.'*

*W*hen King Hassan rudely announced that he was leaving her banquet on board *Britannia* before it was over, the Queen told him that he wouldn't be going anywhere until Beating Retreat had been played. When eventually he was allowed to go, the Queen saw him off from the top of the gangplank. Reaching the shore, the king had the nerve to turn in the expectation of a friendly final wave. But no such luck. The Queen wasn't there; she hadn't bothered to wait.

*A*wkward conversation was being made at Buckingham Palace during the State Visit of General de Gaulle and his wife. Somebody asked Madame de Gaulle what she was most looking forward to in her retirement, which was imminent. With great elaboration, not speaking English much at all, she replied, 'A penis.' Consternation reigned for some time but it was the Queen herself who came to the rescue. 'Ah, happiness,' she said.

*J*ourneying to Balmoral by car, the Queen decreed a comfort stop for her corgis. From the roadside she spied a little shop and thought it would be amusing to buy something from it. Luckily she had her composure, for the shopkeeper said, 'You look awfully like the Queen.' She replied, 'How very reassuring!'

*I*n the 1950s the newly widowed Queen Mother kept on falling over. Unkind rumours began to circulate as to why. At these times, she was an odd spectacle, bucketing around in a wheelchair with the wounded foot bound but the other sporting a shoe with a massive, but temporarily redundant, five inch heel. Eventually people realised, it was the over-ambitious high heels that were the cause of the trouble.

Queen Mary's visits to country houses were dreaded by their owners. It was understood that if she took even a glancing interest in an antique it was hers. In this manner, she acquired, among other things, a priceless Queen Anne cupboard. She was not without scruples, however. So that the whole thing might be looked upon as a swap, she sent the people something in return, something equivalent – a tin tray which, as she explained in the accompanying letter, 'I bought myself from a stall in Benares.'

*A*rriving on her last visit abroad, aged about 85, the Queen Mother took nearly fifteen minutes to descend the aircraft steps. The gloved and hand bagged welcoming party on the tarmac became increasingly uncomfortable but the Queen Mother was unperturbed. Periodically she would pause on the steps and, looking nowhere in particular, give a little twinkle or a half-wave, suggestive perhaps of greater things to come. Upon finally reaching the ground, she looked up, appeared utterly surprised to notice the welcoming party, and was wreathed in smiles.

When she was prime minister, Margaret Thatcher was troubled to find that, at a reception, both she and the Queen were wearing green. She sent a note round the next day: would it be an idea if the two ladies were to confer about their outfits in future? When the reply came it said, 'The Queen does not notice what other people are wearing.'

The Queen posting a letter was intended as the highlight of a ceremony at the Bull Ring in Birmingham. The Queen had the letter ready but, sadly, there was no sign of a postbox. So she posted it into her hand-bag instead.

With Top People

❧

After portraying the Queen with uncanny brilliance in the stage version of Alan Bennett's *A Question of Attribution*, Prunella Scales found herself at Buckingham Palace to collect a CBE. 'I suppose you think you ought to be doing this,' said the true Queen as she pinned on the medal.

Will we ever get to the bottom of what the Queen and Mrs Thatcher really thought of one another? The wife of a prominent politician once came upon the pair in the ladies at a party. The Queen was sitting on the windowsill and the two of them were whispering and giggling and muttering girlishly behind their hands in the most delightfully conspiratorial manner.

$\mathcal{A}$t a State Opening of Parliament in the 1980s, Lord Havers, then Lord Chancellor, was not very quick off the mark. At the head of the procession, he did not move off in time and had to be whacked on the back by the Garter King of Arms who was standing behind him. Afterwards the Queen was in very high spirits. She singled out Garter and said, 'I loved the great biff you gave the Lord Chancellor.' Nor did her good mood end there. As she drove out from the Victoria Tower, in her fur-trimmed state gown and with George IV's diadem on her head, she was spotted pulling funny faces at the Duke of Edinburgh.

Prime ministers have been notoriously cagey about what goes on at the Tuesday audiences with the Queen. But Harold Macmillan let slip that, when John Glenn was orbiting in space in the early 1960s, he and the Queen were so glued to the wireless that affairs of State were overlooked.

Richard Crosman, the Labour minister, made disparaging remarks about the monarchy to Lord Porchester, the Queen's racing manager. The next time he saw the Queen, she opened the conversation menacingly: 'Lord Porchester has been telling me about you.'

When Harold Wilson asked leave of the Queen to go to France, she giggled. The papers had been full of stories of how President Giscard d'Estaing was in the habit of driving about in a car full of spirited women. The Queen pretended to be concerned that Wilson would get mixed up in this too. On his return, the merciless ribbing continued for some time.

Dignitaries arriving at Balmoral in wet weather are sometimes told that now isn't the best time. The footman might gesture to a solitary figure sitting hunched under an umbrella in the middle of the lawn. Often they do not recognise the Queen, picnicking alone while the soft, warm rain of Scotland that she loves falls around her.

When Gore Vidal went swimming in the unwholesome, slimy pool at Royal Lodge with Princess Margaret, the pair found that some unfortunate bees were drowning in the water. So they picked them up and flung them into the air. 'Go forth and make honey,' Princess Margaret barked regally as they buzzed away.

At the Guildhall lunch for her 100th birthday, the Queen Mother was quick to pounce when the Archbishop of Canterbury picked up her glass by mistake. 'That's mine,' she said, snatching it back.

Diana Cooper, the socialite and beauty, was immensely short-sighted and quite used to sustaining conversation with people she could not recognise even though they plainly knew her. But on one occasion she got a shock. She found herself talking to a small woman who was most solicitous and, alarmingly, seemed to know her well. Only by dint of much squinting and peering, did she manage to make out that it was the Queen. Amidst gales of apology and belated curtsying, she said, 'I'm so sorry, I didn't recognise you without your crown on.'

When Hugh Scanlon of the TUC lunched with the Queen in the 1960s, he managed to project a roast potato from his plate on to the floor. It looked as if his hostess had not noticed and, what was more, one of the corgis was approaching and would surely consume it. But the corgi, taking its time, made a lengthy inspection and then wad-

dled away. 'It's not your day, is it?' remarked the Queen.

The Duke and Duchess of Beaufort had the democratic idea of inviting the vicar to dinner with the Queen at Badminton. However they didn't think to tell him that an invitation for 8.30 actually meant 8.15, so the vicar arrived to be greeted by a butler in a flap saying, 'The Queen is just coming down. If you hurry you'll just be in time.' So he hurried, slipped on a wet step and got covered in mud. When he was presented to the Queen, the Duchess said, 'Look at the state he's in.' It was left to the Queen to suggest sponges and make light.

A Labour minister in Harold Wilson's government, called to Balmoral for a Privy Council Meeting, felt uncomfortable when he saw that all the other ministers were in appropriate Scottish wear and he wasn't. But the Queen was charming. Pointing at his chest, she commented, 'How useful a string vest is.'

*G*uests were taking it in turns to spend a few minutes chatting on the sofa with the Queen Mother after dinner. When a well-known actor came up, she was especially animated. 'We know each other well,' she cried and patted a place beside her for him to sit down. They talked about mutual acquaintances and so forth. Then the Queen Mother inquired about his work. He explained he was doing a one-man show that was going on a short tour before ending up at the Edinburgh Festival. 'Which theatre?' asked the Queen Mother. The actor frowned. 'You won't know it, ma'am. It's just a little place.' 'Go on, try me!' 'Well, there's a waxworks attached — it's just a tiny little place …' But the Queen Mother had already risen out of her seat. 'Know it?' she cried. 'I'm in it!'

Out and About

❧

At Sandringham there was a display of prize rabbits. Unfortunately one of them was sadly substandard, in fact a disgrace – nearly bald and scrawny. The lady-owners of the beautiful, sleek rabbits tried to conceal the horrid one from view as the Queen Mother approached. But to no avail. She homed straight in on the wretched creature, picked it up, stroked it, murmured tender words in its ear and exchanged sympathetic glances with its triumphant owner. The other ladies were not best pleased.

When he was Leader of the Opposition in the 1980s, Michael Foot got into hot water about his coat. His knee-length reefer jacket, even though it came from Jaeger, was not thought suitable for the Remembrance Day service at the Cenotaph. But the Queen

Mother made a point of being sympathetic. 'It's an awfully nice coat ... a very sensible coat to wear on a day like this.' Perhaps she was moved by the same spirit that made her pick out the bald rabbit.

But even the Queen Mother could be a little naughty on engagements. Visiting the Royal College of Music, she was introduced to a student. 'What instrument do you play?' she began. 'The violin, ma'am,' he replied. 'I do so like the piano. Such an agreeable instrument, don't you think? ... what an excellent choice,' was the Queen Mother's strange response. As she was leaving she made a point of returning to this student. 'I've never really cared for the violin ... what do you think? ... I'm so glad you chose the piano ... such a wise choice.'

A county lady was once visiting a well-known boutique in London's West End, when she realised that the person riffling through the racks next to her was the Queen. She was so astonished that she wet herself. The Queen had to be led away in helpless laughter and encouraged to sit down on the back stairs. When she had recovered enough to speak, she said, 'It happens so often.'

Princess Diana was always determined to be the first in at Harvey Nichols on a Saturday morning. She would arrive fifteen minutes before opening and pass the time lolling against the taxis in the rank outside and chatting to the drivers.

London was sweltering in a heatwave when the Oliver Messel Exhibition opened. As the designer and social figure, Nicky Haslam, made to embrace Princess Margaret, she stepped back. 'No kissing, Nicky, far too hot.'

When offered a choice of champagne or dry martini by Colin Clark, the younger son of Sir Kenneth, the Queen Mother said, 'They look so delicious, I'll have both.'

One year the Queen Mother gave a party at a villa she had taken in Provence. It was all most romantic – moonlight, olive groves, fountains. After she had retired, she decided to serenade the departing guests on her mouth organ. So, hidden behind a curtain at her bedroom window, she began to play. The effect was magical. The guests were bewitched by this plaintive sound, coming from they knew not where or whom. One of them, in fact, was moved to respond on a horn.

A senior figure at Smithfield meat market relates that, when the Queen Mother and the Duchess of Devonshire visited, he thought it proper to leave them to have some time alone in his office. When the two women emerged, they were full of jolly complaint. They had tried all the cupboards, some of them were locked. Those that were open were a disappointment. They had tried the locked ones again. They had hunted for the key. They had thought they might have to force them open. What had they been looking for?

A woman who had just been splattered with mud by the passing royal car shouted at its occupants. 'I quite agree with you, madam,' said the Queen. The Duke of Edinburgh, who had not heard the woman's remark, asked his wife what she had said. 'Bastards!' said the Queen simply.

*I*n his youth, Theo Aronson, now a highly regarded royal biographer, became entangled with an ironing board in the middle of the road as the Queen Mother's car was bearing down. It screeched to a halt and the bejewelled figure within lurched forward. But by the time he had scrambled out of the way and the car set off again, she was in stitches.

*O*ccasionally, even royalty are reduced to silence. The artist Maggie Hambling, who brooks no nonsense, was introduced to Princess Margaret at an AIDS charity evening at the Royal Academy in the 1980s.

She couldn't remember what to call her, so settled on 'Marg'. Then she said, 'What are you doing surrounded by all these feminists?' 'These are my ladies-in-waiting,' replied Princess Margaret stiffly. Things were not going especially well, but Maggie Hambling was determined to outstay her welcome. This was because Princess Margaret was smoking illegally and, of course, unhindered. As long as she was in the presence, Hambling reckoned, then she could too, if only she could keep on talking. So she started up a topic which was a favourite with her at the time. 'What do you think of *The Singing Detective*, ma'am?' Princess Margaret looked disgusted. 'Isn't that the one about the man with a skin disease? We don't like it.' 'Oh, but it's a masterpiece,' replied Maggie Hambling and began a diatribe which lasted for three-quarters of an hour.

*P*rince Charles's line of questioning on formal occasions can be surprising. He once

asked a soldier, whose young and attractive wife was also present, if they had any children. The soldier replied that they did not but they were keeping their fingers crossed. Prince Charles explained that that was not how babies are made.

The *Daily Telegraph* prepared for a Royal Visit by lavishly dispensing free holidays to those journalists who could not be counted on to behave. Accordingly, the Queen was received with sobriety and hushed murmurs and the visit seemed to be going smoothly.

That is, until one of the unreliables came lurching back from the pub where he had evidently been spending his day off. The Queen immediately jettisoned the toadies and fell into intimate conversation with the red-faced rebel. When gentle inquiries were made, the Queen revealed that they had had a fascinating discussion about the financing of the Royal Train, then, as now, a highly controversial subject.

On her way to the theatre, the Queen was surprised in Windsor High Street by an Italian waiter, who, with many extravagant compliments, presented her with a single rose. 'What a lovely surprise!' the Queen said. Hours later, when she was leaving the theatre, she was still clutching the flower.

Leaning out of the Royal Box at Epsom to an unknown member of the public, the Queen said, 'Oh, look there's my friend. He kissed my hand the other day.'

Princess Margaret and Lord Plumb ignored the 'Keep off the grass' signs while strolling along the Backs at Cambridge. From a distance an acquaintance of the Princess spotted a furious groundsman approaching the pair who, plainly not having identified his victim, was about to make a scene. Scurrying up to deflect him, the acquaintance engaged the Princess in polite conversation: 'How nice to see you out,' etc. Princess Margaret surveyed the scene. 'I'm so glad to see *the people* enjoying themselves,' she declared.

On a visit to a school, Princess Margaret asked the headmistress if she could smoke. The headmistress could hardly say no, but since schools are not naturally set up for smoking there was no ashtray to hand. Nervously staff watched as the ash of the Princess's cigarette grew longer and longer and more and more precarious. In the end, one of the senior staff felt that she had no choice but to rush up and hold out her own hands to become perhaps the first living ashtray.

At Home

Royal staff often take advantage of the facilities. On one occasion two artistic young footmen took over the Queen's private sitting room at Sandringham. They became very excited and set about playing show tunes on the piano, singing and eating the Queen's Bendick's mints. But suddenly they were aware of a presence in the doorway. It was Her Majesty. She stood there for some moments, then went away. The incident was never referred to subsequently.

A well-known male ballet dancer once dined with Princess Margaret. After dinner she announced that she wished to dance and it turned out that what she really wanted was to be lifted high in the air. The task would not have been difficult to accomplish were it not for the complication of the Royal corset. Try as he might, it was impossible to get a grip.

When at last the police arrived to relieve the Queen after she had held out alone against Michael Fagan for the best part of ten minutes, quite naturally, on seeing Her Majesty and before doing anything else, they began to adjust their ties. For the Queen, this was the last straw. 'For goodness sake, get a bloody move on,' she hissed.

The actor Tom Courtenay played a revolutionary in *Doctor Zhivago* and at the time of the film's release was invited to lunch at Buckingham Palace. So nervous was he, he rolled up into a ball and tried to hide behind a sofa. 'Oh, dear,' said the Queen, 'to look at him now, you wouldn't think he wanted to overthrow society, would you?'

When homophobia was raging in the press in the early 1980s, the Queen Mother whispered to a friend before a Palace dinner, 'We think they're marvellous. And besides, if we didn't have any here, we'd have to go self-service.'

Visitors at Clarence House were often mystified by a school-like bell that would ring all over the house at a certain point in the evening. 'Oh, it means the Queen Mother is going to bed,' staff would explain nonchalantly.

Princess Diana invited a little disabled boy, whom she had met through one of her charities, and his parents to tea at Kensington Palace. As small children do, he wandered off and returned some time later laden with armfuls of soft toys — fluffy cats with pink ears, stripy tigers, a polar bear and so on. 'Ah,' she said, 'I see you've found my bedroom.'

One afternoon the Queen Mother asked one of her senior servants what she was supposed to be doing. It seemed that she wasn't doing anything. 'Well, we'll get the car out. I want to see your garden.' 'You mean now?' said the servant, thinking that, apart from anything else, the other inmates of his house in Tooting might be enjoying their afternoon snooze. But the Queen Mother was adamant and off they went. On arrival an elderly neighbour was leaning against the garden fence. 'Your Majesty, may I present Mrs—?' said the servant as the woman's jaw dropped. The next day another inhabitant approached the Queen Mother's attendant. 'I must have been dreaming,' he said, 'but I could swear I saw the Queen Mother in the street yesterday.'

A nervous young officer became even more so when he found himself sitting next to the Queen at lunch. When bread sticks were offered, the Queen took six. In desperation, he did the same. The Queen ate one of her bread sticks. The officer followed suit. The lunch proceeded; the Queen's other bread sticks remained untouched. The officer rearranged his a few times. By the end of the main course, with the whole bread stick situation unresolved, the officer was at his wits' end. Then, with the pudding, the corgis came in. The Queen took up her spare bread sticks and distributed them amongst her dogs. When she had done that and every last crumb had been hoovered up by the animals, she turned to the officer and asked, 'Now, what are you going to do with yours?'

*B*efore a State Dinner at Buckingham Palace, the Queen Mother, the Queen and Princess Margaret prepared to ascend by lift to the bedroom floor in order to put on their evening gowns and jewels. The lift came up from below and the doors opened. Within was an unusual sight. Two footmen were wearing all the jewels that had been ordered for the evening – tiaras, necklaces, brooches, the lot. 'I think they might suit us rather better than you,' the Queen Mother remarked.

A young woman was just beginning to enjoy talking to the Queen at a Buckingham Palace garden party when her mobile phone went off. She was covered in confusion. 'You'd better answer that,' the Queen said. 'It might be someone important.'

*I*n the 1970s a well-meaning but possibly hysterical friend told the Queen Mother that Harrods were going to sack all their homosexual staff. 'What and go self-service?' she replied simply.

*I*nstructed by Palace press secretaries, at Prince Charles's 50th birthday party at Buckingham Palace, not to speak to any member of the Royal Family and not to hover trying to pick up titbits, Jennie Bond thought her only friend would be fellow Royal Correspondent, Nick Owen. Until, that is, she heard a familiar voice nearby. 'Oh look, Mummy. There are *those* two. They're *always* on television. Let's go and say hello.' The Queen and Queen Mother weren't doing as they were told.

*I*n the 1960s, a footman of the Queen Mother's got into trouble for some misdemeanour involving another man and had to leave her service. In the car, as he left Clarence House, he found a bunch of flowers to which was attached a message. 'Who's been a naughty boy, then?'

Just Like Us

~

Often, as she returns from her weekend at Windsor on a Monday morning, the Queen is held up by traffic. On one occasion she was waiting patiently in a great queue in Hyde Park when she became aware of a commotion behind her. She peered round to see blue flashing lights, police mounted on motorcycles and, in the middle of it all, an important limousine being escorted up the clear side of the road in the wrong direction. Who could it be? As the car flashed by, the Queen caught the unmistakable big hair and noble profile of Princess Michael of Kent.

'I don't find it easy myself,' the Queen remarked to some women on a housing estate who were complaining that they couldn't keep their floors clean.

The Royal Family are now obliged to share the beach at Holkham in Norfolk, where they have a beach hut, with nudists. The Queen Mother took an enlightened view, telling Lord Gowrie that 'When the nudists see me, they scamper away into the dunes with their dear little white bottoms fluttering.'

Trying on clothes one day in her middle years, the Queen became skittish. A particular black dress, not her usual taste, entranced her. She pinned on a diamond brooch and flung a mink stole over her shoulder. Standing before the mirror in a Jean Harlow pose, she said, 'Now, if only someone would ask me to something really smart.'

At a jewellery fair at Grosvenor House, the Queen Mother approached a stall holder and pointed to a gigantic brooch. 'I've got one like that at home,' she said.

The owner of an exclusive fabric shop in a run-down part of London was used to seeing great ladies picking their way from their limousines, through the cabbage leaves scattered on the pavement, and into his shop. But it was something of a surprise to come from his back office and find the Princess of Wales sprawled on the floor and the contents of her handbag strewn about her. On entering she had somehow lost her footing and gone flying. She insisted on picking up the lipstick, comb, keys and so forth herself.

Germaine Greer was appalled while on holiday in Greece to learn that she was destined to dine with Princess Margaret who was staying nearby. She hadn't a thing to wear and her hair was a mess. When she arrived, Professor Greer found herself subject to solicitous attention. 'Use my room, if you want to tidy your hair,' Princess Margaret said. In the room was an array of silver-backed brushes. As Greer hesitated, not daring to touch them, Princess Margaret materialised behind her, a little like Jeeves, it would seem. 'Come on, let me help you,' the Princess said, and taking up the brushes and combs, set about tending to the iconoclast's ravaged hair.

In old age, Queen Mary had a few regrets. One of them, which she confided in the Queen Mother, was that she had never climbed over a fence.

Sir Owen Morshead, the Royal Librarian at Windsor, revealed that, in the 1950s, the Queen became interested in Marilyn Monroe. One day she mused, 'I wonder what it must be like to be the most famous woman in the world.'

'Did you find it all right?' inquired the Queen as she greeted one of Prince Charles's girlfriends at Windsor Castle.

During the last war, Queen Mary used to give lifts to young soldiers. She found such contact with ordinary people most interesting.

It is not recorded what the soldiers thought – one moment trudging along the road, the next in the back of a Daimler with Queen Mary.

The Family of Nations

∽

*I*n the 1970s President Giscard d'Estaing telephoned the Queen with a friendly warning about the Ceauşescus, who had just been on a State Visit and were heading to her next. The Queen had better keep an eye on her small valuables! The guests had also behaved as if the Elysée Palace were some kind of cash-and-carry paradise where everything was free. They had ordered lavish quantities of household goods to take home with them. They would probably do the same at Buckingham Palace, if not prevented. Which they were.

*A*t the French Embassy in London there was once an embarrassing clash of national values. The Queen wanted the window open; President Giscard d'Estaing wanted it shut. While the president's back was turned, the Queen ordered that the window be opened. When the Queen wasn't looking, the President had it shut again. This went on all night.

*M*ahatma Gandhi's wedding present to Princess Elizabeth, a piece of white cloth he had woven himself, aroused the darkest suspicions of the Queen Mother and Queen Mary. What if it were a loincloth? But really they needn't have bothered. As Queen, Elizabeth cannot escape visiting countries where loincloths or less are considered ideal formal attire. In South Africa, in 1995, she was greeted at a function in New Brighton by a near-naked praise singer whose spear-waving and singing became more and more frenzied. In the midst of it, the Queen whispered to the BBC's Royal Correspondent, Jennie Bond, 'I *do* hope he's friendly.'

When, in 1953, the Queen was received in Papua New Guinea by the foreign minister he was wearing a suit such as might be seen in the West. But this was not to last. Later he appeared in a grass skirt but only when he stood up did it emerge that the skirt was incomplete. Sitting behind him, the Queen had a prime view of his naked behind with one of the pages of his speech stuck to it.

Early in the reign at the end of a gruelling day during a tour of the United States, the Queen and the Duke of Edinburgh were seated ceremonially on a dais. The Queen whispered to the Duke, 'I'm just so tired, I think I'll keel over at any minute.' The Duke replied, 'Never mind, my little petal, you'll soon be tucked up with the bunnies.'

Imagine their horror when they heard roars of laughter all around them, quite plainly in reaction to what they had said. In their exhaustion, they had forgotten that they were visiting a home for the deaf and dumb. They were surrounded by lip-readers.

Touring South Africa, the Queen Mother met an Afrikaner who was determined to resist her floral charms. 'I'll never forgive the English for what they did to my country,' was the best he could manage. 'But I feel just the same,' said the Queen Mother. 'I'm Scottish and I'll never forgive the English for what they did to my country.'

The Emir of Kuwait gave the Queen a fabulous three-strand pearl necklace when she visited in 1979. In return he got a salver worth about £150.

When We Were Young

~

As a little girl, the Queen was taken by her grandmother, the late Queen Mary, to a concert. Observing her wriggling after the interval, Queen Mary suggested that she might like to go home. 'Oh, no, Granny, just think of all those people waiting to see me outside.' The little princess was immediately removed through a rear exit.

The Archbishop of Canterbury once ruffled the 7-year-old Princess Elizabeth's hair and said, 'How is the little lady?' The Princess replied, 'I'm not a little lady, I'm a Princess.' Queen Mary intervened. 'You were born a Princess. I hope one day that you will be a lady.'

When the Queen was young, her governess, driven to distraction by her pert charge, decided that she would not be on speaking terms. Whenever Princess Elizabeth addressed her, she did not reply. After this had been going on for some time, the Princess said, 'But you can't do this. It's Royalty speaking.'

In an attempt to give them a flavour of normal life, Miss Crawford, the nanny, used to take Princesses Elizabeth and Margaret on various outings around London. But when they went to tea at the Young Women's Christian Association in Great Russell Street, they got rather more normality than they'd bargained for. Princess Elizabeth was unable to grasp the rudiments of self-service and left her teapot on the counter. She got an earful from the tea lady.

At Windsor during the war girls in the same Girl Guide troop as Princess Elizabeth and Princess Margaret noticed the frequency with which they played that memory game where you get a glimpse of a trayful of items and then, when it has been whisked away, you have to recall as many of them as you can. Some even went so far as to complain. Then it was explained that it was all for the sake of the Princesses: a good memory would be vital in their Royal lives and this was a sure way to achieve one.

*A*ged sixteen, Princess Elizabeth approached her duties with all the dangerous enthusiasm of the young. In 1942, after inspecting troops, she reported some soldiers for having dirty engines and they were put on a charge. Later this thorough approach was dropped.

*I*n Kenya, just before she became Queen, Princess Elizabeth was in a fix. Walking through the bush, her car half a mile away and the ladder to her tree house still fifty yards ahead, she found herself in dangerous proximity to a herd of furious elephants. But she forged on regardless.

*C*ynthia Gladwyn, ambassadress to Paris in the early 1950s, had taken a great deal of trouble to find young people, at the last minute, to amuse Princess Margaret during her stay at the embassy. But on the Sunday morning, Princess Margaret was laying claim to a cough, although, the ambassadress couldn't help noticing, it did seem to be oddly intermittent. Nevertheless she couldn't possibly go out and Cynthia Gladwyn was left to visit all the disappointed people without her. Imagine her astonishment, on her return, to find Princess Margaret equipped with a magnificent new coiffure. It was the ambassadress's own maid who revealed the truth. The celebrated hairdresser, Alexandre, had visited the embassy while she was out. This had, in fact, been the plan all along. The next day, after enduring another evening of Princess Margaret's on and off coughing, Cynthia Gladwyn couldn't restrain herself from saying, 'I do hope having your hair shampooed didn't make your cough worse.'

When she first came to the throne the Queen was very reluctant to put on any part of the Crown jewels – she would not contemplate even *one* of the massive diamond necklaces or pairs of earrings. Eventually, to pass a dull afternoon and because the evil day could not be put off for ever, she agreed to have the whole collection brought round from the Tower of London. First she tried on the dainty single rows of diamonds, and slowly built up to the more weighty pieces. At last, decked out in the Imperial State Crown, a huge lumpy necklace, earrings like diamond scythes and the coronation amulets, she dared to look in the mirror. There was a prolonged silence. At last she said, 'Golly'.

We Are Family

❧

The wife of the foreign secretary of the day, Susan Crosland tells of the Queen's robust qualities on a 1970s State Visit. They were aboard *Britannia* during a fierce storm. The Queen had to fight her way into the drawing room, because the door kept sliding shut in her face. Once in, she announced, 'Philip's not at all well ... I'm glad to say.'

It was chicken Kiev for lunch one day at Buckingham Palace. The Queen sensed an opportunity for bad behaviour. She whispered to Michael Foot, 'If you're clever how you put the knife in, you might be able to squirt Philip.'

As a boy, Prince Charles once fell into a sheep dip. As a result he turned red and Princess Anne has made him blush about it ever since.

In the mid-1980s, a passer-by saw Princess Diana examining some postcards outside a shop in Kensington High Street. Nothing very remarkable about that. But when she called her detective over and together they began to point and giggle, the onlooker naturally wanted to know what was so funny. When they had gone, he went to investigate. What he found were postcards of the Queen wearing a tiara, another of her mounted on a horse with her corgis and ones of Prince Charles in various uniforms and also in gumboots, leaning on an alpenstock.

The Queen's idea of appropriate dress for cuddling her babies? Nothing at all. It seemed perfectly natural to her, she explained while she was sitting for a sculptor and they were discussing the shape and texture of the human body. But when the newspapers got to hear of it, it was, of course: 'Queen's nude romps with her children.'

People always say that the Duke of Edinburgh needs an outlet, but is he really so very different from other men? He always has to have the latest gadget and on one occasion it was an electric fryer. This had the additional advantage of indulging the passion more peculiar to royalty for doing your own cooking. But the Queen did not care to find the smell of fried sausages still in the dining room at lunchtime and that was the end of the electric fryer.

Devotedly the Duke of Edinburgh set about converting a Victorian silver teapot into an electric kettle for the Queen. The idea was that she could enjoy the thrill, student-style, of making her own tea in her room. But when the Duke wheeled a portable forge into the drawing room after dinner and sparks began to fly all over the upholstery, the Queen had to banish him to more suitable premises.

During a demure Lenten visit to the Deanery at Windsor, the Queen sipped tomato juice and soon made her excuses. Half an hour later Princess Margaret appeared. Following precedent, she was offered some more of the seasonal tomato juice. 'Good God no!' she said. 'Get out the whisky.' She did not leave for some time.

Somebody once complained to Princess Margaret that the Queen had been hard work at a state dinner. 'That's what she's there for,' she replied.

Princess Margaret had her doubts about her paternal grandmother. She considered Queen Mary's slavish devotion to the ideal of monarchy rather vulgar and a somewhat pathetic attempt to make up for not really being Royal herself, which she wasn't – quite – by birth.

The Queen Mother was always concerned that her daughter, the Queen, should never find out that she used tea bags.

The Queen Mother is only known to have made one faintly bitchy remark. She didn't really like Edwina Mountbatten, Lord Mountbatten's ritzy and somewhat wide-ranging wife. When she heard that Edwina had been buried at sea, she said, 'Poor Edwina, she did always like to make a splash.'

*V*isiting your family tombs may seem like an odd way to entertain visitors, but this is how things are done in the Royal Family. During an amble around St George's Chapel, Windsor, a collection of guests passed by the side-chapel where George VI is buried. 'The King, you know,' the Queen Mother remarked conversationally, 'he's in there.' Then she added, 'And I shall be too, one day.' Later the Queen was heard to say, 'She doesn't mind, you see, she really doesn't mind at all.'

The Duchess of Windsor and the Queen Mother were supposed to have been daggers drawn for years, so there was some curiosity when, at the funeral of her husband, the two met face to face. But the duchess merely inquired, 'Is your kitchen upstairs or downstairs?' If the Queen Mother was confused, she didn't show it. The duchess continued for some time to explain the virtues of an upstairs kitchen before the Queen Mother could deftly extract herself. It was only towards the end of the wake that the Queen Mother once again found the rather terrifying, stick-thin, improbably youthful figure of the duchess at her side. Evidently her first reply had been unsatisfactory because the duchess asked again, 'Is your kitchen upstairs or downstairs?'

At a ball the Queen Mother was dancing with a young subaltern when she was called away. Upon her return she discovered her partner was now dancing with the Queen. Biding her time, she found, or had found for her, a new partner and relaunched herself on to the dance floor. Round and round they went, until at last the pattern of the dance brought her near the rival couple. 'Snob!' she whispered in the ear of the original partner.

A curious exchange was overheard by waiting celebrities as the Queen and the Queen Mother arrived at a West End theatre. 'Who do you think you are?' the Queen Mother was saying. 'The Queen, Mummy, the Queen.'

When the Queen was about to open Sandringham to the public, she confided to guests at Badminton during pre-lunch drinks, 'Mummy is simply furious with me for doing it.'

At Epsom, the Queen remarked that she hadn't watched a race through binoculars for years and that doing so now had caused tears to stream down her face. The Queen Mother said dryly, 'Perhaps it's all the emotion,' whereupon the Queen became rather shrill: 'No, Mummy, you know perfectly well … when you're standing in the wind …'

One day, contemplating her mother's limitless wardrobe, the Queen said, 'I'll never know why she wants all these dresses. They're all the same.'

Arriving at a picnic hut on the Balmoral estate, the Queen found herself unable to gain entrance. She hadn't got the right key. Returning to the castle to fetch it, she came across her mother, who was less than sympathetic. 'How very odd! Darling, I thought, if it was you, all you had to say was "Open Sesame".'

Climbing one of the Matopo Hills in South Africa in order to reach the grave of Cecil Rhodes, the then Princess Elizabeth had to surrender her sandals to her mother and continue barefoot. The Queen's high heels were hopeless for mountain climbing. 'So like Mummy,' Princess Elizabeth remarked, 'to set out in those shoes.'

Making Do

~

Whereas many of us will write a message on our hand if there is something we really must remember, the Queen writes hers on her glove.

A couturier was advising the Queen which hat to wear with her new outfit. He suggested one that she had worn some years earlier. 'I don't know that I could find it now,' she said, but eventually agreed to see what she could do. Being pressed further, she said, 'All right, we'll see.' The couturier was led through many miles of passages at Buckingham Palace until they reached a remote attic. 'Try up there,' the Queen said. The couturier stood on a chair and lifted down the box that the Queen had indicated. Inside was the hat.

A similar incident occurred with Queen Mary in the 1920s, when George V was very ill. The doctor asked for moistened cloths to be hung over the windows of the King's bedroom to keep the air clean. Queen Mary said, 'I know just the thing' and conducted the doctor on a long tour through the palace to a remote attic, perhaps the same one. It contained lengths of fabric that had belonged to Queen Victoria which was just what he wanted.

The Queen always has a jigsaw on the go. She likes those 1,000 piece ones with lots of sky. To save expense, and besides they are of no interest once done and only take up room, the Queen hires them from a jigsaw club at a cost of £30 a year.

*I*t is very annoying to the Queen that her dinner service at Windsor, which dates from George III, is missing four items. She often mentions it to her guests: once there were 280 pieces, now only ...

*D*uring audiences with the Queen, people are sometimes aware that Her Majesty is making unaccountable sideways movements with her hands. But since she keeps her gaze trained perfectly on her interlocutor, they never get the chance to peer over and find out more. Thus they never see that the Queen's jigsaw is surreptitiously laid out on a low table beside her chair – in case inspiration should strike without warning.

*T*he Queen is not, perhaps, a nurturer of plants, but she is an irrepressible weeder. At Balmoral she will spend hours tugging and wrenching in the borders.

When Prince Charles lost a dog lead at Sandringham, the Queen insisted that he go back and find it. 'Dog leads cost money!' the Queen informed her son matter-of-factly.

In the 1960s the Queen lost her watch while out for a walk at Sandringham. For two weeks subsequently an entire battalion of the army was set to comb the ground looking for it, which they never did.

If people were having Princess Margaret round, they tended to put themselves out. But the trouble was the longer the trail of catering vans outside the house, the greater the range and complication of the sauces, then the more she craved simplicity. Shown a sumptuous supper room with little gilt chairs hired for the occasion, she would say, 'I don't want to go in there. I'd rather have something on a tray by the fire. How about a boiled egg?' For the senior diplomats, captains of industry, the great and the good of every description who were present never was there such a testing hour as when they had to coax Princess Margaret to her seat and save a party from ruin.

When Colin Clark was filming Prince Charles's interview with Alistair Cooke at Windsor, the three of them stopped for lunch. Only there wasn't any. Prince Charles explained that, of the Royal Family, only the Queen had the power to command lunch at Windsor. There was plenty of lunch for all the castle staff of course, but royalty, on this occasion, had to make do with chicken sandwiches out of a Tupperware box, which had been brought down from London.

When Prince Charles first went to prep school he got a stomach upset. This was apparently on account of the 'rich' food at the school, quite unlike what was offered at home.

$\mathcal{A}$t school, Prince Charles asked to be sent a toy boat because all the other boys had got one. But when it arrived it was by far the smallest.

$\mathcal{M}$eeting Francis King at a Society of Authors party at the Mansion House, Prince Charles said, 'Snap!' and pointed downwards. They were wearing identical shoes. King had bought his in a sale at Russell and Bromley. What could this mean?

$\mathcal{E}$ntertaining celebrity chefs at home is as daunting for the Queen as it would be for the rest of us. When Ruth Rogers of the River Café, which was once voted the best restaurant in Europe, came to lunch at Buckingham Palace, the Queen said: 'I know it's not what you're used to.'

$\mathcal{D}$uring one of her intimate lunches for top people, the Queen said to one guest, 'Now, you really must say if anything is not to your liking.' Later it emerged that this person was an expert on wine. The Queen said, 'What do you think of this?' holding up her glass. The guest, mindful of her previous words, said that it could be improved upon. The Queen said, 'I'll see what I can do' and a certain amount of murmuring with the butler ensued. A different bottle was produced for this visitor's approval, which was given. When the butler had filled his glass, he made to offer some to the other guests, but the Queen said, 'No, no, it's just for Mr—.'

The Queen has never encouraged any fancy ways in her children. 'Will it wash?' she inquired of a piece of fabric when Princess Anne's wedding trousseau was being prepared.

Visitors to the College of Arms are sometimes shown a tatty old polythene bag. They are astonished when told that the cushion it contains is the one that the Queen sat on at her Coronation.

The Queen once tried to order a picnic basket from Peter Jones by telephone. The exercise would have been a failure had not the sceptical assistant who took her call thought to check with Buckingham Palace afterwards. A governessy member of the household tutted and muttered words to the effect that the Queen really ought to know better.

The Queen Mother used to enjoy dining at the Temple. And no wonder. The cellars are legendary and, of course, nothing but the very best was lavished on her. Nevertheless at the end of one dinner, when a priceless Château Yqem was offered, she startled her hosts by saying, 'Do you know, I think just a few more glasses of the champagne we had to start with would do perfectly.'

When huffy, no-nonsense novelist Evelyn Waugh suddenly conceived a mania to meet the exquisitely floral Queen Mother, nobody could quite understand why. But a meeting was arranged in a flat somewhere and the hostess produced champagne. The Queen Mother was girlish and enchanting. 'Oh, champagne,' she exclaimed, waving her arms about, 'what a treat!' Evelyn Waugh remained stiffly immobile while his face assumed a look of uncompromising disbelief: 'A treat, ma'am?' It is not recorded how the encounter progressed after that.

*I*n the 1950s the Queen Mother visited Sissinghurst for both lunch and tea. Afterwards a courtier reported that she had been charmed by the simplicity of the arrangements. Harold Nicolson was rather put out. 'SIMPLE indeed! When I think of my Kümmel, the Moselle wine, and the truffles!'

*D*uring the last summer of her life, Princess Diana took frequent flights on a friend's private jet and became friendly with the staff on board. On one occasion, as she entered the aircraft on a Friday having returned to London only four days before, she said breathlessly, 'I've *just* managed to get the washing done in time.' Diana was often observed by her friends doing her own ironing.

*I*n her latter years, Princess Margaret, it is said by some, renounced the exclusive, high fashion ways of her youth. She became simple in her tastes. Kitty Kelley, the terrifying scourge of the Windsors, describes the sad spectacle of a cheap folding table propped up against a wall in the drawing room of Princess Margaret's apartment, used, she was informed, for the Princess's solitary TV dinners. Others claim to have seen her, of an afternoon, enjoying a leisurely mooch around Ikea on the North Circular Road.

*P*rices were never mentioned in any discussion between Norman Hartnell and the Queen Mother about her clothes. But on one occasion, he thought it wise to warn her that the osprey feathers she was contemplating cost £100 (and this was in 1960). She became rather still and her jaw jutted just a little. Then she said, 'In that case, I'll have another set in white.'

*I*t emerges that the balcony at Clarence House is not equipped for Royal appearances. The Queen Mother used to wave from it on her birthday but she had to stand on an upturned flowerpot in order to be seen at all.

*A*t the end of the war, Dame Jocelyn Woollcombe, Director of the Wrens, received the Queen, later Queen Mother, at her headquarters. The Queen disappeared into the ladies and re-emerged in a state of high excitement. 'You must go and wash your hands,' she said to her lady-in-waiting, 'they've got Elizabeth Arden soap!'

$\mathcal{A}$t lunch at Kensington Palace (it was 'an Indian' in fact but presumably not 'take-away') Princess Margaret banged on her poppadom and bits flew all over the room. Her polite guest was half-way out of his seat to pick them up, when she said, 'Don't do that.' She indicated the butler. 'That's what he's there for.'

$\mathcal{T}$he Queen Mother's staff at Clarence House were treated in unconventional ways. A number of them had their own apartments in the building, the kitchens of which – because food was provided in the staff dining room – remained unused. A senior member of staff, however, one day found his kitchen mysteriously stocked up with jars of olives, tins of pâté, boxes of fondant creams, Bendick's mints and quantities of cheese footballs. He made inquiries and found that the trail led back to the Queen Mother herself. 'I thought you might want to give a dinner party,' she explained.

*S*he was also ahead of her time in the matter of the home delivery of food. Years before ordinary people had fallen into the habit of telephoning to restaurants for dishes to be biked round, she would insist, if she heard that a member of her staff had been invited out to dinner, that the Clarence House kitchen should provide everything and that it should be conveyed to the party, with the guest, in a royal car.

*T*he Queen Mother once confessed to a friend that she often had a small drink before going out in the evening. Indeed, often, she would have another, and then, equally often, she would have another one after that. 'And, do you know,' she said, 'it doesn't have any effect at all.'

Our Best Friends

~

Before the Queen travels abroad she leaves detailed instructions in her own hand, complete with maps, as to where her dogs are to be taken for their walks. There is a different route for each day.

When the Queen is naming her horses, which she does herself, her flair for puzzles and crosswords is much in evidence. Her rule is that the name must reflect the parentage of the horse. Thus she arrived at Church Parade for the offspring of Queen's Hussar and Christchurch and Round Tower for a filly 'by' High Top 'out of' Circlet. When the parents were Amnesia and Lord Elgin, Lost Marbles was the perfect choice.

*T*wo horses returned from Ireland. The Queen spotted at once that something was amiss. Doutelle had been accidentally renamed Agreement and Agreement had turned into Doutelle. Nobody else had noticed.

'*C*ome here, you little bugger!' the Queen exclaimed at Balmoral to an escaping corgi. She was restored to graciousness when a guest of one of the staff shoved the animal back through a hole in the fence for her.

$\mathcal{A}$ friend of the Queen's received a letter of condolence from Her Majesty on the death of her mother. It was typewritten and occupied one side of the paper. When this same friend's Labrador died, however, she got six sides of handwriting.

$\mathcal{W}$hen the couturier, Ian Thomas, first started to design for the Queen, he was annoyed that the corgis would run off with his samples of fabric or roll all over them or chew them up. But eventually he found that he could use the animals to his advantage. By dint of a little strategic placing, he could see to it that the samples the corgis got hold of were the ones he didn't want the Queen to choose.

$\mathcal{C}$orgis really are rather difficult animals, despite, in the case of the Queen's pets, the attentions of the animal psychologist, Dr Roger Mugford. Once, in Windsor Great Park, the Queen could not persuade one especially awkward one to get back into the car after its walk. At first it sat stubbornly on the grass, then, despite repeated, very clear orders, it actually went so far as to go and sit under the vehicle. But the Queen knew exactly what to do. She got back into the car herself and ordered it to drive on. It was, of course, the perfect way to flush the wretched animal out.

*I*t is well known that the Queen feeds her dogs with great ceremony – silver bowls, finest tartan rugs, etc. What is less well known is that she feeds them in order of dog precedence.

When the Queen's corgi, Crackers, became decrepit and unable to walk, a special dog wheelchair was constructed for him.

The Royal Family have been animal lovers since Queen Victoria's day but none of them have gone quite as far as Queen Alexandra. When her Pekinese, Togo, died in 1914, she was beside herself. She refused to have the corpse removed but kept it in her bedroom, where she would 'look at it and sob'. After two days the smell was such that the lady-in-waiting was 'nearly knocked down' on entering the room. She pleaded with the Queen to have the dead dog removed. High officials were involved and expressed grave concern. But nobody could do anything. Eventually egg sandwiches appeared at tea. The Queen smelt them. Tearfully, she said, 'Just like my sweet little Togo.' This caused an outbreak of hysteria in the lady-in-waiting. Soon Queen Alexandra caught it too. Demented laughter raged for some time. Then the lady-in-waiting got a grip on herself sufficiently to seize the initiative. 'For goodness sake, ma'am, have him removed or I shall never be able to look at an egg again.'

'All right,' conceded the Queen at last. At once the lady-in-waiting was in the corridor, giving the order to a passing page.

*I*n the 1990s, Clarence House was rigged up with every kind of digital and cable TV so that the Queen Mother could watch the racing. A surprise consequence of this was that she became mad about the dogs. On one occasion there was great agitation because a horserace at Doncaster had over-run and it was looking as if the 3.51 from Catford wouldn't be shown.

*P*resenting the Gold Cup at the Cheltenham Races, the Queen Mother chatted at length with the jockey but she talked to the horse the longest.

We Are Amused

~

*I*n order to relieve the tedium of sitting for her portrait, the Queen commandeers a room at the front of Buckingham Palace overlooking the Mall. Sneakily she arranges to sit near the window. 'Isn't the light better?' she inquires innocently of the painter. But her object is really to be diverted by the tourists below. The real fun comes when they think they've seen *her*. Often she keeps up a running commentary. 'No, they can't believe it.' 'They're coming back for another look.' 'Their jaws have absolutely dropped a mile.'

The Queen Mother was sitting alone in regal splendour (she was *never* informally dressed, even in bed), waiting for a repeat of *Dad's Army* to begin. But her gin and Dubonnet had not arrived, so she telephoned down to the servants' quarters. 'I don't know what you old queens are doing down there,' she said, 'but this old queen is getting rather thirsty.'

Joining the Queen Mother on a bench in Diana Cooper's drawing room, Lady Freda Berkeley was alarmed to find that the effect of her sitting down was to send the Queen Mother soaring into the air. Dismounting proved impossible and the two ladies spent nearly five minutes see-sawing up and down, whooping with girlish yet gracious delight.

The catering staff at Cheltenham Race Course were doing their best to manage in a tiny kitchen. One of them, sensing the door open behind her, said forthrightly, 'You can't come in here. There isn't room to swing a cat.' It was only at this point that she chose to look round – to find the Queen Mother, blinking in the doorway. She thought to herself, 'This is a Tower job, at the very least.' But the Queen Mother was unperturbed. 'Oh, yes,' she said, 'I can see that you are rather cosy,' and was gone.

During the First World War an officer was busy with paperwork in his room not far behind the front line. When someone opened his door and appeared to hang about indecisively, the officer snapped, 'Come in or go out, but shut the bloody door.' This produced no effect so, too pre-occupied to look up, he tried again, 'Come in or go out, but shut the bloody door.' Still no reaction. He tried a third time, and only then did he think to look up, to find His

Majesty George V, rather nonplussed, gazing down on him. Years later, when this officer was given an honour, the King remembered him well. 'Come in or go out, but shut the bloody door,' was his opening remark at the investiture.

$\mathcal{A}$ stable girl at Windsor saw out of the corner of her eye somebody apparently at a loose end in the stable yard. 'Go and fetch some water!' she commanded. A few moments later she turned round to see the Queen trotting up obediently bearing a full pail.

$\mathcal{A}$s the Investiture of the Prince of Wales was about to begin, the Queen cried out at a sudden jabbing pain in her side. For a moment it was feared Charles would become King rather sooner than he had bargained for. Upon investigation, it turned out that a pin had been left in her frock.

$\mathcal{A}$t a grand reception at the Victoria and Albert Museum, Princess Margaret's right arm swung up, it swung down, and up it swung again. Onlookers began to wonder if the rumours that Royalty are sometimes asleep and being worked mechanically were in fact true. Then someone noticed that the hand on the end of the agitated arm held an empty glass. The Princess was expressing her desire for more whisky. This was all very well but sadly she had had her meagre ration and there was none.

*A*fter a film premiere Lady Elizabeth Cavendish, John Betjeman, Princess Margaret, Prince Charles and Lord Snowdon convened in a private room at Rules Restaurant in Covent Garden. When Prince Charles had to leave early, Lady Elizabeth Cavendish, as the hostess, accompanied him to the street door, going barefoot because she had kicked off her shoes during dinner. While she was out of the room, Princess Margaret retrieved the shoes from under the table and placed them on Lady Elizabeth's plate.

*A*lan Clark watched the Queen Mother's 90th Birthday Parade from a balcony with Princess Margaret and Prince Charles. It struck him as odd that Prince Charles should block his aunt's view and that she should not protest. Only when the Prince moved suddenly and was sharply told by the Princess to resume his previous position, did Clark work out what she was up to. In order that she should be able to smoke throughout the parade, her first priority was to be screened from the photographers, even if that meant that she could see nothing herself. Bad Princess Margaret.

Antonio Carluccio once got into a slight muddle in the presence of Princess Margaret. He explained that he had been picking mushrooms with 'your brother'. What he meant was 'your nephew', Prince Charles. But Princess Margaret was not at all put out. 'You've made my day,' she said, patting her hair becomingly.

When Lord Woodrow Wyatt was propounding his interesting theory that the reason so many spies emanated from Cambridge rather than Oxford was because Cambridge was a dead-end town and not even the train went on anywhere after it, Princess Margaret soon put him in his place. 'Yes, it does,' she said. 'It goes to Sandringham.'

At the laying of the foundation stone of the National Theatre, it was noticed that the Queen Mother held her bouquet at some distance from her nose. Enchantingly it contained specimens of all the flora mentioned in Shakespeare, including a leek, a dock leaf, bogwort and rank fumitory.

In extreme old age, the Queen Mother teamed up with Sir Stephen Runciman, who was also magnificently ancient. She used to like dining at his club, the Athenaeum and her absolutely favourite moment came, when, on the way to the loo, she would say to her escort, 'Come on, do let's.' Then, blazing with naughtiness, she would open the door of the men-only sitting room, pop her head in for just long enough to observe the rumbling discomfiture of the grandees within, before flitting away.

Coming together into the auditorium at Covent Garden, Sir Frederick Ashton and the Queen Mother received a rapturous reception. 'Don't they just love us old queens!' the Queen Mother whispered to Ashton.

When the Queen Mother came to lunch, Diana Cooper would often assemble a collection of unmarried and uninhibited clergy for drinks beforehand. On one occasion, as she was leaving, the Queen Mother remarked to her hostess, 'I did enjoy your bouquet of clergy.'

Patrons of The Arts

At the famous Post Impressionist Exhibition at the Grafton Gallery, George V contemplated a Cezanne. His wife was on the other side of the room. 'Come over here, May,' he bellowed, 'there's something that will make you laugh.' Later his loathing for this artist's pictures reached such a pitch that he attacked the frame of one with his stick.

The Queen does not like the opera, nor the ballet for that matter. But in 1977, Jubilee Year, a visit to Covent Garden was unavoidable. Courtiers tried to make helpful suggestions. 'How about *The Marriage of Figaro*?' 'Is that the one with the pin?' she asked. 'Yes,' they said, fearing the worst. 'I've seen it,' said the Queen terminally.

Rising at the end of a performance of *Don Quixote*, Princess Margaret said, 'Brenda would have liked the donkey.' It seems Brenda is not only *Private Eye*'s name for Her Majesty the Queen.

On her rare visits to the opera, the Queen is not always treated with kid gloves. Lord Drogheda once made a speech from the stage in which he said, 'Now that Her Majesty has found the way, perhaps she will come more often to the opera.'

The Kennedys and the Windsors did not really have much in common. During a rather sticky formal dinner, Gore Vidal recounts, the Queen suddenly said to Jackie Kennedy, 'You like Art, don't you?' Before she knew what was happening Mrs Kennedy found herself hurtling through room after room at Buckingham Palace, past fabulous Titians, Rembrandts and goodness knows what. Only in front of a Van Dyck did they pause for the Queen to say, 'That's a good horse,' before charging on.

Princess Margaret was a mistress of the flat contradiction. When Derek Granger, the well-known film producer, escorted her into the theatre to see *Anything Goes*, he remarked that the recorded singer they could hear was Cole Porter. It was hardly such a controversial thing to say. The show was after all by Cole Porter and there was even a huge photograph of him in place of the curtain. Besides he was quite certain.

But Princess Margaret didn't see it like that. 'No, it isn't,' she said. 'I know Cole Porter's voice and that's not it.' Then she said, 'By the way, you're standing on my frock.' In the second half Derek Granger found himself replaced as the Princess's neighbour by Sir Ian McKellen.

$\mathcal{A}$t the World Travel Market at Olympia in 1987, the artist Richard Walker had to present his prize-winning picture to Princess Anne. It so happened that it was very large and seeing him struggling up on to the stage with it, she said, 'I bet you wouldn't have done it so big if you'd known you were going to have to lug it round all day.'

$\mathcal{G}$eorge V told Sir Thomas Beecham that he liked *La Bohème*: 'It's the shortest one I know.' He couldn't even bring himself to use the word 'opera'.

*I*n the late 1970s, to gain inspiration for her décor at Windsor, the Queen visited one of the hotels at Heathrow Airport.

*H*er Majesty does not consider it her place to comment on any theatrical performance she might have seen – even when it has been as monumental and unsurpassed as Maria Callas's *Tosca* of the early 1960s. But the Queen did, however, go so far as to remark on the prettiness of her frock when she met the diva afterwards.

*T*he Queen was once greatly exercised when a number of bishops took to wearing scarlet cassocks. It would seem that the Queen has an ancient right to pronounce on ecclesiastical modes. She complained that they looked like 'something out of a Fellini film', referring presumably to the outrageous, ecclesiastical fashion show at the end of *Roma*. How astonishing that she had even heard of such a film.

*I*n her old age, Queen Mary, long known for her unbending regality, took to visiting the New Lindsey Theatre in Kensington, which favoured more challenging work. Here she saw *Pick-up Girl*, an American play about adolescent sex and VD.

*A*t the end of a performance of *Romeo and Juliet* at the ballet, Derek Granger was in the midst of correctly thanking Princess Diana for coming and so on when she interrupted. 'Oh, nonsense,' she said, 'I'm delighted to be here. What do you think I'd be doing otherwise?' This was a question Derek Granger didn't feel able to answer. 'I'd be at home with a tray on my knees watching *EastEnders*.'

*A*s they were going in to the premiere of *Where Angels Fear to Tread*, Princess Diana remarked to its producer: 'You must have seen it so many times. Why don't you go to sleep and I'll wake you up at the end.'

*I*t was at a party hosted by Maureen Dufferin and Ava, that Princess Margaret's performance of 'My Old Man's a Dustman' was subject to heckling. Somebody shouted, 'Shut up, you old bag.' Horrified guests turned round to see the artist, Francis Bacon, very much the worse for wear.

Sources

Aronson, Theo, *Royal Subjects*, Sidgwick & Jackson, London 2000

Bond, Jennie, *Reporting Royalty*, Headline, London 2001

Brown, Craig and Leslie Cunliffe, *Book of Royal Lists*, Sphere Books Ltd, London 1983

Clark, Alan, *Diaries*, Weidenfeld and Nicolson, London 1993

Clark, Colin, *The Prince, The Showgirl and Me*, the Colin Clark Diaries, HarperCollins, London 1994

    — *Younger Brother, Younger Son: A Memoir*, HarperCollins, London 1998

De-la-Noy, Michael, *The Queen Behind the Throne*, Hutchinson, London 1994

Gladwyn, Cynthia, *The Diaries of Cynthia Gladwyn*, Constable, London 1995

Kelly, Kitty, *The Royals*, Warner Books, New York 1997

Hastings, Selina, *Evelyn Waugh, a Biography*, Sinclair Stevenson, London 1994

Lacey, Robert, *Royal: Her Majesty Queen Elizabeth II*, Little Brown, London 2002

Lees-Milne, James, *Ancestral Voices*, Chatto & Windus, London 1975

    — *Prophesying Peace*, Chatto & Windus, London 1977

    — *Harold Nicolson, A Biography* (Vol. II), Chatto & Windus, London 1981

    — *Caves of Ice*, Chatto & Windus, London 1983

    — *Midway on the Waves*, Faber, London 1985

    — *A Mingled Measure*, John Murray, London 1994

    — *Ancient as the Hills*, John Murray, London 1997

    — *Through Wood and Dale*, John Murray, London 1998

    — *Deep Romantic Chasm*, John Murray, London 2000

    — *Holy Dread*, John Murray, London 2001

Longford, Elizabeth, *Elizabeth R: A Biography*, Weidenfeld and Nicolson, London 1983

Morrow, Ann, *The Queen*, Panther, London 1984

Olivier, Laurence, *Confessions of an Actor*, Weidenfeld and Nicolson, London 1982

Rose, Kenneth, *King George V*, Macmillan, London, 1987

Vidal, Gore, *Palimpsest: A Memoir*, Andre Deutsch, London 1995

Wyatt, Woodrow, *The Journals of Woodrow Wyatt*, Macmillan, London 1999–2000

Zieger, Philip, *Diana Cooper*, Hamish Hamilton, London 1981